Robert Green Ingersoll

A Thanksgiving sermon

Robert Green Ingersoll

A Thanksgiving sermon

ISBN/EAN: 9783337266110

Printed in Europe, USA, Canada, Australia, Japan

Cover: Foto ©Lupo / pixelio.de

More available books at **www.hansebooks.com**

A
THANKSGIVING SERMON

BY

ROBERT G. INGERSOLL.

ALSO,

A TRIBUTE TO HENRY WARD BEECHER

I thank the heroes, the apostles of reason, the disciples of truth, the soldiers of freedom—the heroes who held high the holy torch and filled the world with light.

C. P. FARRELL, PUBLISHER,
NEW YORK,
1897.

Entered according to Act of Congress, in the year 1897,
By C. P. FARRELL,
In the Office of the Librarian of Congress at Washington, D. C.

The Eckler Press
35 Fulton St.
New York.

A THANKSGIVING SERMON.

MANY ages ago our fathers were living in dens and caves. Their bodies, their low foreheads, were covered with hair. They were eating berries, roots, bark and vermin. They were fond of snakes and raw fish. They discovered fire and, probably by accident, learned how to cause it by friction. They found how to warm themselves—to fight the frost and storm. They fashioned clubs and rude weapons of stone with which they killed the larger beasts and now and then each other. Slowly, painfully, almost imperceptibly they advanced. They crawled and stumbled, staggered and struggled towards the light. To them the world was unknown. On every hand was the mysterious, the sinister, the hurtful. The forests were filled with monsters and the darkness was crowded with ghosts, devils, and fiendish gods.

These poor wretches were the slaves of fear, the sport of dreams.

Now and then, one rose a little above his fellows—used his senses—the little reason that he had—found something new—some better way. Then the people killed him and afterwards knelt with reverence at his grave. Then another thinker gave his thought—was murdered—another tomb became sacred—another step was taken in advance. And so through countless years of ignorance and cruelty—of thought and crime—of murder and worship, of heroism, suffering, and self-denial, the race has reached the heights where now we stand.

Looking back over the long and devious roads that lie between the barbarism of the past and the civilization of to-day, thinking of the centuries that rolled like waves between these distant shores, we can form some idea of what our fathers suffered—of the mistakes they made—some idea of their ignorance, their stupidity—and some idea of their sense, their goodness, their heroism.

It is a long road from the savage to the scientist—from a den to a mansion—from leaves to clothes—from a flickering rush to the arc-light—from a hammer of stone to the modern mill—a long distance from the pipe of Pan to the violin—to the orchestra—from a floating log to the steamship—from a sickle to a reaper—from a flail to a threshing machine—from a crooked stick to a plow—from a spinning wheel to a spinning jenny—from a hand loom to a Jaccard—a Jaccard that weaves fair forms and wondrous flowers beyond Arachne's utmost dream—from a few hieroglyphics on the skins of beasts—on bricks of clay—to a printing press, to a library—a long distance from the messenger, traveling on foot, to the electric spark—from knives and tools of stone to those of steel—a long distance from sand to telescopes—from echo to the phonograph, the phonograph that buries in indented lines and dots the sounds of living speech, and then gives back to life the very words and voices of the dead—a long way from the trumpet to the telephone, the telephone that transports speech as swift as thought and drops the words, perfect as minted coins, in listening ears—a long way from a fallen tree to the suspension bridge—from the dried sinews of beasts to the cables of steel—from the oar to the propeller—from the sling to the rifle—from the catapult to the cannon—a long distance from revenge to law—from the club to the legislature—from slavery to freedom—from appearance to fact—from fear to reason.

And yet the distance has been traveled by the human race. Countless obstructions have been overcome—numberless enemies have been conquered—thousands and thousands of victories have been won for the right and millions have lived, labored and died for their fellowmen.

For the blessings we enjoy—for the happiness that is ours, we ought to be grateful. Our hearts should blossom with thankfulness.

Whom, what, should we thank?

Let us be honest—generous.

Should we thank the church?

Christianity has controlled christendom for at least fifteen hundred years.

During these centuries what have the orthodox churches, accomplished for the good of man?

In this life man needs raiment and roof, food and fuel. He must be protected from heat and cold, from snow and storm. He must take thought for the morrow. In the summer of youth he must prepare for the winter of age. He must know something of the causes of disease—of the conditions of health. If possible he must conquer pain, increase happiness and lengthen life. He must supply the wants of the body—and feed the hunger of the mind.

What good has the church done?

Has it taught man to cultivate the earth? to build homes? to weave cloth? to cure or prevent disease? to build ships, to navigate the seas? to conquer pain, or to lengthen life?

Did Christ or any of his apostles add to the sum of useful knowledge? Did they say one word in favor of any science, of any art? Did they teach their fellowmen how to make a living—how to overcome the obstructions of nature, how to prevent sickness—how to protect themselves from pain, from famine, from misery and rags?

Did they explain any of the phenomena of nature? any of the facts that affect the life of man? Did they say anything in favor of investigation—of study—of thought? Did they teach the gospel of self-reliance, of industry—of honest effort? Can any farmer, mechanic, or scientist find in the New Testament one useful fact? Is there anything in the sacred book that can help the geologist? the astronomer? the biologist, the physician, the inventor—the manufacturer of any useful thing?

What has the church done?

From the very first it taught the vanity—the worthlessness of all earthly things. It taught the wickedness of wealth, the blessedness of poverty. It taught that the business of this life was to prepare for death. It insisted that a certain belief was necessary to insure salvation, and that all who failed to believe, or doubted in the least would suffer eternal pain. According to the church the natural desires, ambitions and passions of man were all wicked and depraved.

To love God—to practice self-denial—to overcome desire—to despise wealth—to hate prosperity—to desert wife and children—to live on roots and berries—to repeat prayers—to wear rags—to live in filth and drive love from the heart—these, for centuries were the highest and most perfect virtues and those who practiced them were saints.

The saints did not assist their fellowmen.

Their fellowmen assisted them. They did not labor for others. They were beggars—parasites—vermin. They were insane. They followed the teachings of Christ. They took no thought for the morrow. They mutilated their bodies—scarred their flesh and destroyed their minds for the sake of happiness in another world. During the journey of life they kept their eyes on the grave. They gathered no flowers by the way—they walked in the dust of the road—avoided the green fields. Their moans made all the music they wished to hear. The babble of brooks, the songs of birds, the laughter of children, were nothing to them. Pleasure was the child of sin, and the happy needed a change of heart. They were sinless and miserable—but they had faith—they were pious and wretched—but they were limping towards heaven.

What has the church done?

It has denounced pride and luxury—all things that adorn and enrich life—all the pleasures of sense—the ecstacies of love—

the happiness of the hearth—the clasp and kiss of wife and child.

And the church has done this because it regarded this life as a period of probation—a time to prepare—to become spiritual—to overcome the natural—to fix the affections on the invisible—to become passionless—to subdue the flesh—to congeal the blood—to fold the wings of fancy—to become dead to the world—so that when you appeared before God you would be the exact opposite of what he made you.

What has the church done?

It pretended to have a revelation from God. It knew the road to eternal joy, the way to death. It preached salvation by faith, and declared that only orthodox believers could become angels, and all doubters would be damned. It knew this, and so knowing it became the enemy of discussion, of investigation, of thought. Why investigate, why discuss, why think when you know? It sought to enslave the world.

It appealed to force. It unsheathed the sword, lighted the fagot, forged the chain, built the dungeon, erected the scaffold, invented and used the instruments of torture. It branded, maimed and mutilated—it imprisoned and tortured—it blinded and burned, hanged and crucified, and utterly destroyed millions and millions of human beings. It touched every nerve of the body—produced every pain that can be felt, every agony that can be endured.

And it did all this to preserve what it called the truth—to destroy heresy and doubt, and to save, if possible, the souls of a few. It was honest. It was necessary to prevent the development of the brain—to arrest all progress—and to do this the church used all its power. If men were allowed to think and express their thoughts they would fill their minds and the minds of others with doubts. If they were allowed to think they would investigate, and then they might contradict the creed, dispute the words of priests and defy the church. The priests cried to the people: "It is for us to talk. It is for you to hear. Our duty is to preach and yours is to believe."

What has the church done?

There have been thousands of councils and synods—thousands and thousands of occasions when the clergy have met and discussed and quarrelled—when pope and cardinals, bishops and priests have added to or explained their creeds—and denied the rights of others. What useful truth did they discover? What fact did they find? Did they add to the intellectual wealth of the world? Did they increase the sum of knowledge?

I admit that they looked over a number of Jewish books and picked out the ones that Jehovah wrote.

Did they find the medicinal virtue that dwells in any weed or flower?

I know that they decided that the Holy Ghost was not created—not begotten—but that he proceeded.

Did they teach us the mysteries of the metals and how to purify the ores in furnace flames?

They shouted: "Great is the mystery of Godliness."

Did they show us how to improve our condition in this world?

They informed us that Christ had two natures and two wills.

Did they give us even a hint as to any useful thing?

They gave us predestination, foreordination and just enough "free will" to go to hell.

Did they discover or show us how to produce anything for food?

Did they produce anything to satisfy the hunger of man?

Instead of this they discovered that a peasant girl who lived in Palestine, was the mother of God. This they proved by a book, and to make the book evidence they called it inspired.

Did they tell us anything about chemistry—how to combine and separate substances—how to subtract the hurtful—how to produce the useful?

They told us that bread, by making certain motions and mumbling certain prayers, could be changed into the flesh of God, and that in the same way wine could be changed to his blood. And this, notwithstanding the fact that God never had any flesh or blood, but has always been a spirit without body, parts or passions.

What has the church done?

It gave us the history of the world—of the stars, and the beginning of all things. It taught the geology of Moses—the astronomy of Joshua and Elijah. It taught the Fall of man and the atonement—proved that a Jewish peasant was God—established the existence of Hell, Purgatory and Heaven.

It pretended to have a revelation from God—the Scriptures, in which could be found all knowledge—everything that man could need in the journey of life. Nothing outside of the inspired book—except legends and prayers—could be of any value. Books that contradicted the Bible were hurtful, those that agreed with it—useless. Nothing was of importance except faith, credulity—belief. The church said: "Let philosophy alone, count your beads. Ask no questions, fall upon your knees. Shut your eyes, and save your souls."

What has the church done?

For centuries it kept the earth flat—for centuries it made all the hosts of heaven travel around this world—for centuries it clung to "sacred" knowledge and fought facts with the ferocity of a fiend. For centuries it hated the useful. It was the deadly enemy of medicine. Disease was produced by devils and could be cured only by priests, decaying bones and holy water. Doctors were the rivals of priests. They diverted the revenues.

The church opposed the study of anatomy —was against the dissection of the dead. Man had no right to cure disease—God would do that through his priests.

Man had no right to prevent disease—diseases were sent by God as judgments.

The church opposed innoculation—vaccination, and the use of chloroform and ether. It was declared to be a sin, a crime for a woman to lessen the pangs of motherhood. The church declared that woman must bear the curse of the merciful Jehovah.

What has the church done?

It taught that the insane were inhabited by devils. Insanity was not a disease. It was produced by demons. It could be cured by prayers—gifts, amulets and charms. All these had to be paid for. This enriched the church. These ideas were honestly entertained by Protestants as well as Catholics— by Luther, Calvin, Knox and Wesley.

What has the church done?

It taught the awful doctrine of witchcraft.

It filled the darkness with demons—the air with devils, and the world with grief and shame. It charged men, women and children with being in league with Satan to injure their fellows. Old women were convicted for causing storms at sea—for preventing rain and for bringing frost. Girls were convicted for having changed themselves into wolves, snakes and toads. These witches were burned for causing diseases—for selling their souls and for souring beer. All these things were done with the aid of the devil who sought to persecute the faithful, the lambs of God. Satan sought in many ways to scandalize the church. He sometimes assumed the appearance of a priest and committed crimes.

On one occasion he personated a bishop—a bishop renowned for his sanctity—allowed himself to be discovered and dragged from the room of a beautiful widow. So perfectly did he counterfeit the features and form of the bishop, that many who were well acquainted with the prelate, were actually deceived, and the widow herself thought her lover was the bishop. All this was done by the devil to bring reproach upon holy men.

Hundreds of like instances could be given, as the war waged between demons and priests was long and bitter.

These popes and priests—these clergymen, were not hypocrites. They believed in the New Testament—in the teachings of Christ, and they knew that the principal business of the Savior was casting out devils.

What has the church done?

It made the wife a slave—the property of the husband, and it placed the husband as much above the wife as Christ was above the husband. It taught that a nun is purer, nobler than a mother. It induced millions of pure and conscientious girls to renounce the joys of life—to take the veil woven of night and death, to wear the habiliments of the dead—made them believe that they were the brides of Christ.

For my part I would as soon be a widow as the bride of a man who had been dead for eighteen hundred years.

The poor deluded girls imagined that they, in some mysterious way, were in spiritual wedlock united with God. All worldly desires were driven from their hearts. They filled their lives with fastings—with prayers—with self-accusings. They forgot fathers and mothers and gave their love to the invisible. They were the victims, the convicts of superstition—prisoners in the penitentiaries of God. Conscientious, good, sincere—insane.

These loving women gave their hearts to a phantom, their lives to a dream.

A few years ago, at a revival, a fine buxom girl was "converted," "born again." In her excitement she cried, "I'm married to Christ—I'm married to Christ." In her delirium she threw her arms around the neck of an old man and again cried "I'm married to Christ." The old man, who happened to be a kind of skeptic, gently removed her hands, saying at the same time: "I don't know much about your husband, but I have great respect for your father-in-law."

Priests, theologians, have taken advantage of women—of their gentleness—their love of approbation. They have lived upon their hopes and fears. Like vampires, they have sucked their blood. They have made them responsible for the sins of the world. They have taught them the slave virtues—meekness, humility—implicit obedience. They have fed their minds with mistakes, mysteries and absurdities. They have endeavored to weaken and shrivel their brains, until, to them, there would be no possible connection between evidence and belief—between fact and faith.

What has the church done?

It was the enemy of commerce—of business. It denounced the taking of interest for money. Without taking interest for money, progress is impossible. The steamships, the great factories, the railroads have all been built with borrowed money, money on which interest was promised and for the most part paid.

The church was opposed to fire insurance—to life insurance. It denounced insurance in any form as gambling, as immoral. To insure your life was to declare that you had no confidence in God—that you relied on a corporation instead of divine providence. It was declared that God would provide for your widow and your fatherless children.

To insure your life was to insult Heaven.

What has the church done?

The church regarded epidemics as the messengers of the good God. The "Black Death" was sent by the eternal Father, whose mercy spared some and whose justice murdered the rest. To stop the scourge, they tried to soften the heart of God by kneelings and prostrations—by processions and prayers—by burning incense and by making vows. They did not try to remove the cause. The cause was

God. They did not ask for pure water, but for holy water. Faith and filth lived, or rather died together. Religion and rags, piety and pollution kept company.

Sanctity kept its odor.

What has the church done?

It was the enemy of art and literature. It destroyed the marbles of Greece and Rome. Beauty was Pagan. It destroyed so far as it could the best literature of the world. It feared thought—but it preserved the scriptures, the ravings of insane saints, the falsehoods of the Fathers, the bulls of popes, the accounts of miracles performed by shrines, by dried blood and faded hair, by pieces of bones and wood, by rusty nails and thorns, by handkerchiefs and rags, by water and beads and by a finger of the holy Ghost.

This was the literature of the church.

I admit that the priests were honest—as honest as ignorant. More could not be said.

What has the church done?

Christianity claims, with great pride, that it established asylums for the insane. Yes it did. But the insane were treated as criminals. They were regarded as the homes—as the tenement-houses of devils. They were persecuted and tormented. They were chained and flogged, starved and killed. The asylums were prisons, dungeons, the insane were victims and the keepers were ignorant, conscientious, pious fiends. They were not trying to help men, they were fighting devils —destroying demons. They were not actuated by love—but by hate and fear.

What has the church done?

It founded schools where facts were denied, where science was denounced and philosophy despised. Schools, where priests were made —where they were taught to hate reason and to look upon doubts as the suggestions of the devil. Schools where the heart was hardened and the brain shriveled. Schools in which lies were sacred and truths profane. Schools for the more general diffusion of ignorance—

schools to prevent thought—to suppress knowledge. Schools for the purpose of enslaving the world. Schools in which teachers knew less than pupils.

What has the church done?

It has used its influence with God to get rain and sunshine—to stop flood and storm—to kill insects, rats, snakes and wild beasts—to stay pestilence and famine—to delay frost and snow—to lengthen the lives of kings and queens—to protect presidents—to give legislators wisdom—to increase collections and subscriptions. In marriages it has made God the party of the third part. It has sprinkled water on babes when they were named. It has put oil on the dying and repeated prayers for the dead. It has tried to protect the people from the malice of the devil—from ghosts and spooks, from witches and wizards and all the leering fiends that seek to poison the souls of men. It has endeavored to protect the sheep of God from the wolves of science —from the wild beasts of doubt and investigation. It has tried to wean the lambs of the Lord from the delights, the pleasures, the joys of life. According to the philosophy of the church, the virtuous weep and suffer, the vicious laugh and thrive, the good carry a cross, and the wicked fly. But in the next life this will be reversed. Then, the good will be happy, and the bad will be damned.

The church filled the world with faith and crime.

It polluted the fountains of joy. It gave us an ignorant, jealous, revengeful and cruel God—sometimes merciful—sometimes ferocious. Now just, now infamous—sometimes wise—generally foolish. It gave us a devil, cunning, malicious, almost the equal of God, not quite as strong—but quicker—not as profound—but sharper.

It gave us angels with wings—cherubins and seraphim and a heaven with harps and hallelujahs—with streets of gold and gates of pearl.

It gave us fiends and imps with wings like

bats. It gave us ghosts and goblins, spooks and sprites, and little devils that swarmed in the bodies of men, and it gave us hell where the souls of men will roast in eternal flames. Shall we thank the church? Shall we thank the orthodox churches?

Shall we thank them for the hell they made here? Shall we thank them for the hell of the future?

II.

We must remember that the church was founded and has been protected by God, that all the popes and cardinals, all the bishops, priests and monks, all the ministers and exhorters were selected and set apart—all sanctified and enlightened by the infinite God—that the Holy Scriptures were inspired by the same Being, and that all the orthodox creeds were really made by Him.

We know what these men—filled with the Holy Ghost have done. We know the part they have played. We know the souls they have saved and the bodies they have destroyed. We know the consolation they have given and the pain they have inflicted—the lies they have defended—the truths they have denied. We know that they convinced millions that celibacy is the greatest of all virtues—that women are perpetual temptations, the enemies of true holiness—that monks and priests are nobler than fathers, that nuns are purer than mothers. We know that they taught the blessed absurdity of the Trinity—that God once worked at the trade of a carpenter in Palestine. We know that they divided knowledge into sacred and profane—taught that Revelation was sacred—that Reason was blasphemous—that faith was holy and facts false. That the sin of Adam and Eve brought disease and pain, vice and death into the world. We know that they have taught the dogma of Special Providence—that all events are ordered and regulated by God—that he crowns and uncrowns kings—preserves and destroys—guards and kills—that it is the duty of man to submit to the divine will, and that no matter how much evil there may be—no matter how much suffering—how much pain and death, man should pour out his heart in thankfulness that it is no worse.

Let me be understood. I do not say and I do not think that the church was dishonest, that the clergy were insincere. I admit that all religions, all creeds, all priests, have been naturally produced. I admit, and cheerfully admit, that the believers in the supernatural have done some good—not because they believed in gods and devils—but in spite of it.

I know that thousands and thousands of clergymen are honest, self-denying and humane—that they are doing what they believe to be their duty—doing what they can to induce men and women to live pure and noble lives. This is not the result of their creeds—it is because they are human.

What I say is that every honest teacher of the supernatural has been and is an unconscious enemy of the human race.

What is the philosophy of the church—of those who believe in the supernatural?

Back of all that is—back of all events—Christians put an infinite Juggler who with a wish creates, preserves, destroys. The world is his stage and mankind his puppets. He fills them with wants and desires, with appetites and ambitions—with hopes and fears—with love and hate. He touches the springs. He pulls the strings—baits the hooks, sets the traps and digs the pits.

The play is a continual performance.

He watches these puppets as they struggle and fail. Sees them outwit each other and themselves—leads them to every crime, watches the births and deaths—hears lullabies at cradles and the fall of clods on coffins. He has no pity.—He enjoys the tragedies—the desperation—the despair—the suicides. He smiles at the murders, the assassinations,—the seductions, the desertions—the abandoned babes of shame. He sees the weak enslaved—mothers robbed of babes—the innocent in dungeons—on scaffolds. He sees crime crowned and hypocrisy robed.

He withholds the rain and his puppets starve. He opens the earth and they are devoured. He sends the flood and they are drowned. He empties the volcano and they perish in fire. He sends the cyclone and they are torn and mangled. With quick lightnings they are dashed to death. He fills the air and water with the invisible enemies of life—the messengers of pain and watches the puppets as they breathe and drink. He creates cancers to feed upon their flesh—their quivering nerves—serpents, to fill their veins with venom,—beasts to crunch their bones—to lap their blood.

Some of the poor puppets he makes insane—makes them struggle in the darkness with imagined monsters with glaring eyes and dripping jaws and some are made without the flame of thought to drool and drivel through the darkened days.—He sees all the agony, the injustice, the rags of poverty, the withered hands of want—the motherless babes—the deformed—the maimed—the leprous, knows the tears that flow—hears the sobs and moans—sees the gleam of swords, hears the roar of the guns—sees the fields reddened with blood—the white faces of the dead. But he mocks when their fear cometh, and at their calamity he fills the heavens with laughter. And the poor puppets who are left alive, fall on their knees and thank the Juggler with all their hearts.

But after all the gods have not supported the children of men, men have supported the gods. They have built the temples. They have sacrificed their babes, their lambs, their cattle. They have drenched the altars with blood. They have given their silver, their gold, their gems. They have fed and clothed their priests—but the gods have given nothing in return. Hidden in the shadows they have answered no prayer—heard no cry—given no sign—extended no hand—uttered no word. Unseen and unheard they have sat on their thrones, deaf and dumb—paralyzed and blind. In vain the steeples rise—in vain the prayers ascend.

And think what man has done to please the gods. He has renounced his reason—extinguished the torch of his brain, he has believed without evidence and against evidence. He has slandered and maligned himself. He has fasted and starved. He has mutilated his body—scarred his flesh—given his blood to vermin. He has persecuted, imprisoned and destroyed his fellows.—He has deserted wife and child. He has lived alone in the desert. He has swung censers and burned incense, counted beads and sprinkled himself with holy water—shut his eyes, clasped his hands—fallen upon his knees and groveled in the dust—but the gods have been silent—silent as stones.

Have these cringings and crawlings—these cruelties and absurdities—this faith and foolishness pleased the gods?

We do not know.

Has any disaster been averted—any blessing obtained? We do not know.

Shall we thank these Gods?

Shall we thank the church's God?

Who and what is he?

A THANKSGIVING SERMON.

They say that he is the creator and preserver of all that has been—of all that is—of all that will be—that he is the father of angels and devils, the architect of heaven and hell—that he made the earth—a man and woman—that he made the serpent who tempted them, made his own rival—gave victory to his enemy—that he repented of what he had done—that he sent a flood and destroyed all of the children of men with the exception of eight persons—that he tried to civilize the survivors and their children—tried to do this with earthquakes and fiery serpents—with pestilence and famine.—But he failed. He intended to fail. Then he was born into the world, preached for three years and allowed some savages to kill him. Then he rose from the dead and went back to heaven

He knew that he would fail, knew that he would be killed.—In fact he arranged everything himself and brought everything to pass just as he had predestined it—an eternity—

before the world was. All who believe these things will be saved and they who doubt or deny will be lost.

Has this God good sense?

Not always.—He creates his own enemies and plots against himself. Nothing lives, except in accordance with his will, and yet the devils do not die.

What is the matter of this god?—Well, sometimes he is foolish—sometimes he is cruel and sometimes he is insane.

Does this God exist? Is there any intelligence back of Nature?—Is there any Being anywhere among the stars who pities the suffering children of men?

We do not know.—

Shall we thank Nature?

Does Nature care for us more than for leaves, or grass, or flies?

Does Nature know that we exist? We do not know.

But we do know that Nature is going to murder us all.

Why should we thank Nature? If we thank God or Nature for the sunshine and rain, for health and happiness, whom shall we curse for famine and pestilence, for earthquake and cyclone—for disease and death?

III.

If we cannot thank the orthodox churches —if we cannot thank the unknown, the incomprehensible, the supernatural—if we cannot thank Nature—if we cannot kneel to a Guess, or prostrate ourselves before a Perhaps—whom shall we thank?

Let us see what the worldly have done—what has been accomplished by those not "called," not "set apart," not "inspired," not filled with the Holy Ghost—by those who were neglected by all the gods.

Passing over the Hindus, the Egyptians, the Greeks and Romans, their poets, philosophers and metaphysicians — we will come to modern times.

In the 10th century after Christ the Saracens—governors of a vast empire—"established colleges in Mongolia, Tartary, Persia, Mesopotamia, Syria, Epypt, North Africa, Morocco, Fez and in Spain." The region owned by the Saracens was greater than the Roman Empire. "They had not only colleges—but observatories. The sciences were taught. They introduced the ten numerals—taught algebra and trigonometry—understood cubic equations—knew the art of surveying—they made catalogues and maps of the stars—gave the great stars the names they still bear—they ascertained the size of the earth—determined the obliquity of the ecliptic and fixed the length of the year. They calculated eclipses, equinoxes, solstices, conjunctions of planets and occultations of stars. They constructed astronomical instruments. They made clocks of various kinds and were the inventors of the pendulum. They originated chemistry—discovered sulphuric and nitric acid and alcohol.

They were the first to publish pharmacopœias and dispensatories.

In mechanics they determined the laws of falling bodies. They understood the mechanical powers, and the attraction of gravitation.

They taught hydrostatics and determined the specific gravities of bodies.

In optics they discovered that a ray of light did not proceed from the eye to an object—but from the object to the eye."

They were manufacturers of cotton, leather, paper and steel. "They gave us the game of chess." They produced romances and novels and essays on many subjects.

"In their schools they taught the modern doctrines of evolution and development." They anticipated Darwin and Spencer.

These people were not Christians. They were the followers, for the most part, of an impostor—of a pretended prophet of a false God. And yet while the true Christians, the men selected by the true God and filled with the Holy Ghost were tearing out the tongues of heretics, these wretches were irreverently tracing the orbits of the stars. While the true believers were flaying philosophers and extinguishing the eyes of thinkers, these godless followers of Mohammed were founding colleges, collecting manuscripts, investigating the facts of nature and giving their attention to science. Afterwards the followers of Mohammed became the enemies of science and hated facts as intensely and honestly as Christians. Whoever has a revelation from God will defend it with all his strength—will abhor reason and deny facts.

But it is well to know that we are indebted to the Moors—to the followers of Mohammed—for having laid the foundations of modern science. It is well to know that we are not indebted to the Church, to Christianity, for any useful fact.

It is well to know that the seeds of thought were sown in our minds by the Greeks and Romans and that our literature came from those seeds. The great literature of our language is Pagan in its thought—Pagan in its beauty—Pagan in its perfection. It is well to know that when Mohammedans were the friends of science, Christians were its enemies. How consoling it is to think that the friends of science—the men who educated their fellows—are now in hell, and that the men who persecuted and killed philosophers are now in heaven! Such is the justice of God.

The Christians of the Middle Ages, the men who were filled with the Holy Ghost, knew all about the worlds beyond the grave, but nothing about the world in which they lived. They thought the earth was flat—a little dishing if anything—that it was about five thousand years old and that the stars were little sparkles made to beautify the night.

The fact is that Christianity was in existence for fifteen hundred years before there was an astronomer in Christendom. No follower of Christ knew the shape of the earth.

The earth was demonstrated to be a globe, not by a Pope or Cardinal—not by a collection of clergymen—not by the "called" or the "set apart," but by a sailor. Magellan left Seville, Spain, August 10th, 1519, sailed west and kept sailing west, and the ship reached Seville, the port it left, on Sept. 7th, 1522.

The world had been circumnavigated. The earth was known to be round. There had been a dispute between the Scriptures and a sailor. The fact took the sailor's side.

In 1543 Copernicus published his book, "On the Revolutions of the Heavenly Bodies."

He had some idea of the vastness of the stars—of the astronomical spaces—of the insignificance of this world.

Toward the close of the 16th century Bruno, one of the greatest men this world has produced, gave his thoughts to his fellowmen. He taught the plurality of worlds. He was a Pantheist, an Atheist, an honest man. He called the Catholic Church the "Triumphant Beast." He was imprisoned for many years, tried, convicted, and on the 16th day of February, 1600, burned in Rome by men filled with the Holy Ghost, burned on the spot where now his monument rises. Bruno, the noblest, the greatest of all the martyrs. The only one who suffered death for what he believed to be the truth. The only martyr who had no heaven to gain, no hell to shun, no God to please. He was nobler than inspired men, grander than prophets, greater and purer than apostles. Above all the theologians of the world, above the makers of creeds, above the founders of religions rose this serene, unselfish and intrepid man.

Yet Christians, followers of Christ, murdered this incomparable man. These Christians were true to their creed. They believed that faith would be rewarded with eternal joy and doubt punished with eternal pain. They were logical. They were pious and pitiless—devout and devilish—meek and malicious—religious and revengeful—Christ-like and cruel—loving with their mouths and hating with their hearts. And yet, honest victims of ignorance and fear.

What have the worldly done?

In 1608, Lippershay, a Hollander, so arranged lenses that objects were exaggerated.

He invented the telescope.

He gave countless worlds to our eyes—and made us citizens of the Universe.

In 1610, on the night of January 7th, Galileo demonstrated the truth of the Copernicum system, and in 1632 published his work on "The System of the World."

What did the Church do?

Galileo was arrested, imprisoned, forced to fall upon his knees, put his hand on the Bible, and recant. For ten years he was kept in prison—for ten years until released by the pity of death. Then the Church—men filled with the Holy Ghost—denied his body burial in consecrated ground. It was feared that his dust might corrupt the bodies of those who had persecuted him.

In 1609 Kepler published his book "Motions

of the Planet Mars." He, too, knew of the attraction of gravitation and that it acted in proportion to mass and distance. Kepler announced his Three Laws. He found and mathematically expressed the relation of distance, mass, and motion. Nothing greater has been accomplished by the human mind.

Astronomy became a science and Christianity a superstition.

Then came Newton, Herschel and La Place. The astronomy of Joshua and Elijah faded from the minds of intelligent men, and Jehovah became an ignorant tribal god.

Men began to see that the operations of Nature were not subject to interference. That eclipses were not caused by the wrath of God —that comets had nothing to do with the destruction of empires or the death of kings, that the stars wheeled in their orbits without regard to the actions of men. In the sacred East the dawn appeared.

What have the worldly done?

A few years ago a few men became wicked

enough to use their senses. They began to look and listen. They began to really see and then they began to reason. They forgot heaven and hell long enough to take some interest in this world. They began to examine soils and rocks. They noticed what had been done by rivers and seas. They found out something about the crust of the earth. They found that most of the rocks had been deposited and stratified in the water. Rocks 70,000 feet in thickness. They found that the coal was once vegetable matter. They made the best calculations they could of the time required to make the coal, and concluded that it must have taken at least six or seven millions of years. They examined the chalk cliffs, found that they were composed of the microscopic shells of minute organisms, that is to say, the dust of these shells. This dust settled over areas as large as Europe and in some places the chalk is a mile in depth. This must have required many millions of years.

Lyell, the highest authority on the subject, says that it must have required, to cause the changes that we know, at least two hundred million years. Think of these vast deposits caused by the slow falling of infinitesimal atoms of impalpable dust through the silent depths of ancient seas! Think of the microscopical forms of life, constructing their minute houses of lime, giving life to others, leaving their mansions beneath the waves, and so through countless generations building the foundations of continents and islands.

Go back of all life that we now know—back of all the flying lizards, the armored monsters, the hissing serpents, the winged and fanged horrors—back to the Laurentian rocks—to the eozóon, the first of living things that we have found—back of all mountains, seas and rivers—back to the first incrustation of the molten world—back of wave of fire and robe of flame—back to the time when all the substance of the earth blazed in the glowing sun with all the stars that wheel about the central fire.

Think of the days and nights that lie between!—think of the centuries, the withered leaves of time, that strew the desert of the past!

Nature does not hurry. Time cannot be wasted—cannot be lost. The future remains eternal and all the past is as though it had not been—as though it were to be. The infinite knows neither loss nor gain.

We know something of the history of the world—something of the human race; and we know that man has lived and struggled through want and war, through pestilence and famine, through ignorance and crime, through fear and hope, on the old earth for millions and millions of years.

At last we know that infallible popes, and countless priests and clergymen, who had been "called," filled with the Holy Ghost, and presidents of colleges, kings, emperors and executives of nations had mistaken the blundering guesses of ignorant savages for the wisdom of an infinite God.

At last we know that the story of creation, of the beginning of things, as told in the "sacred book" is not only untrue, but utterly absurd and idiotic. Now we know that the inspired writers did not know and that the God who inspired them did not know.

We are no longer misled by myths and legends. We rely upon facts. The world is our witness and the stars testify for us.

What have the worldly done?

They have investigated the religions of the world—have read the sacred books, the prophecies, the commandments, the rules of conduct. They have studied the symbols, the ceremonies, the prayers and sacrifices. And they have shown that all religions are substantially the same—produced by the same causes—that all rest on a misconception of the facts in nature—that all are founded on ignorance and fear, on mistake and mystery.

A THANKSGIVING SERMON.   49

They have found that Christianity is like the rest—that it was not a revelation, but a natural growth—that its gods and devils, its heavens and hells, were borrowed—that its ceremonies and sacraments were souvenirs of other religions—that no part of it came from heaven, but that it was all made by savage man. They found that Jehovah was a tribal god and that his ancestors had lived on the banks of the Euphrates, the Tigris, the Ganges and the Nile, and these ancestors were traced back to still more savage forms.

They found that all the sacred books were filled with inspired mistake and sacred absurdity.

But, say the Christians, we have the only inspired book. We have the Old Testament and the New.—Where did you get the Old Testament? From the Jews?—Yes.

Let me tell you about it.

After the Jews returned from Babylon, about 400 years before Christ, Ezra commenced making the Bible. You will find an account of this in the Bible.

We know that Genesis was written after the captivity—because it was from the Babylonians that the Jews got the story of the Creation—of Adam and Eve, of the Garden—of the serpent, and the tree of life—of the flood—and from them they learned about the Sabbath.

You find nothing about that holy day in Judges, Joshua, Samuel, Kings or Chronicles—nothing in Job, the Psalms, in Esther, Solomon's Song or Ecclesiastes. Only in books written by Ezra after the return from Babylon.

When Ezra finished the inspired book, he placed it in the temple. It was written on the skins of beasts, and, so far as we know, there was but one.

What became of this Bible?

Jerusalem was taken by Titus about 70 years after Christ. The temple was destroyed and, at the request of Josephus, the Holy

Bible was sent to Vespasian the Emperor, at Rome.

And this Holy Bible has never been seen or heard of since. So much for that.

Then there was a copy, or rather a translation, called the Septuagint.

How was that made?

It is said that Ptolemy Soter and his son Ptolemy Philadelphus obtained a translation of the Jewish Bible. This translation was made by seventy persons.

At that time the Jewish Bible did not contain Daniel, Ecclesiastes, but few of the Psalms and only a part of Isaiah.

What became of this translation known as the Septuagint?

It was burned in the Bruchium Library forty-seven years before Christ.

Then there was another so-called copy of part of the Bible, known as the Samaritan Roll of the Pentateuch.

But this is not considered of any value.

Have we a true copy of the Bible that was

in the temple at Jerusalem—the one sent to Vespasian?

Nobody knows.

Have we a true copy of the Septuagint?

Nobody knows.

What is the oldest manuscript of the Bible we have in Hebrew?

The oldest manuscript we have in Hebrew was written in the 10th century after Christ. The oldest pretended copy we have of the Septuagint written in Greek was made in the 5th century after Christ.

If the Bible was divinely inspired, if it was the actual word of God, we have no authenticated copy. The original has been lost and we are left in the darkness of Nature.

It is impossible for us to show that our bible is correct. We have no standard. Many of the books in our bible contradict each other. Many chapters appear to be incomplete and parts of different books are written in the same words, showing that both could not have been original. The 19th and 20th chapters of 2nd Kings and the 37th and 38th chapters of Isaiah are exactly the same. So is the 36th chapter of Isaiah from the 2nd verse the same as the 18th chapter of 2nd Kings from the 2nd verse.

So, it is perfectly apparent that there could have been no possible propriety in inspiring the writers of Kings and the writers of Chronicles. The books are substantially the same, differing in a few mistakes—in a few falsehoods. The same is true of Leviticus and Numbers. The books do not agree either in facts or philosophy. They differ as the men differed who wrote them.

What have the worldly done?

They have investigated the phenomena of nature. They have invented ways to use the forces of the world, the weight of falling water—of moving air. They have changed water to steam, invented engines—the tireless giants that work for man. The have made lightning a messenger and slave. They invented movable type, taught us the art of printing and made it possible to save and transmit the intellectual wealth of the world. They connected continents with cables, cities and towns with the telegraph—brought the world into one family—made intelligence independent of distance. They taught us how to build homes, to obtain food, to weave cloth. They covered the seas with iron ships and the land with roads and steeds of steel. They gave us the tools of all the trades—the implements of labor. They chiseled statues, painted pictures and "witched the world" with form and color. They have found the cause of and the cure for many maladies that afflict the flesh and minds of men. They have given us the instruments of music and the great composers and performers have changed the common air to tones and harmonies that intoxicate, exalt and purify the soul.

They have rescued us from the prisons of fear, and snatched our souls from the fangs and claws of superstition's loathsome, crawling, flying beasts. They have given us the liberty to think and the courage to express our thoughts. They have changed the frightened, the enslaved, the kneeling, the prostrate into men and women—clothed them in their right minds and made them truly free. They have uncrowned the phantoms, wrested the scepters from the ghosts and given this world to the children of men. They have driven from the heart the fiends of fear and extinguished the flames of hell.

They have read a few leaves of the great volume—deciphered some of the records written on stone by the tireless hands of time in the dim past. They have told us something of what has been done by wind and wave, by fire and frost, by life and death, the ceaseless workers, the pauseless forces of the world.

They have enlarged the horizon of the known, changed the glittering specks that shine above us to wheeling worlds, and filled all space with countless suns.

They have found the qualities of substances, the nature of things—how to analyze, separate and combine, and have enabled us to use the good and avoid the hurtful.

They have given us mathematics in the higher forms, by means of which we measure the astronomical spaces, the distances to stars, the velocity at which the heavenly bodies move, their density and weight, and by which the mariner navigates the waste and trackless seas. They have given us all we have of knowledge, of literature and art. They have made life worth living. They have filled the world with conveniences, comforts and luxuries.

All this has been done by the worldly—by those who were not "called" or "set apart" or filled with the Holy Ghost or had the slightest claim to "apostolic succession." The men who accomplished these things were not "inspired." They had no revelation—no supernatural aid. They were not clad in sacred vestments, and tiaras were not upon their brows. They were not even ordained. They used their senses, observed and recorded facts. They had confidence in reason. They were patient searchers for the truth. They turned their attention to the affairs of this world. They were not saints. They were sensible men. They worked for themselves, for wife and child and for the benefit of all.

To these men we are indebted for all we are, for all we know, for all we have. They were the creators of civilization—the founders of free States—the saviors of liberty—the destroyers of superstition—the great captains in the army of progress.

IV.

Whom shall we thank?

Standing here at the close of the 19th century—amid the trophies of thought—the triumphs of genius—here under the flag of the Great Republic—knowing something of the history of man—here on this day that has been set apart for thanksgiving, I most reverently thank the good men, the good women of the past, I thank the kind fathers, the loving mothers of the savage days. I thank the father who spoke the first gentle word, the mother who first smiled upon her babe. I thank the first true friend. I thank the savages who hunted and fished that they and their babes might live. I thank those who cultivated the ground and changed the forests into farms—those who built rude homes and watched the faces of their happy children in the glow of fireside flames—those who domesticated horses, cattle and sheep—those who invented wheels and looms and taught us to spin and weave—those who by cultivation changed wild grasses into wheat and corn, changed bitter things to fruit and worthless weeds to flowers that sowed within our souls the seeds of Art. I thank the poets of the dawn—the tellers of legends—the makers of myths—the singers of joy and grief, of hope and love. I thank the artists who chiseled forms in stone and wrought with light and shade the face of man. I thank the philosophers, the thinkers, who taught us how to use our minds in the great search for truth. I thank the astronomers who explored the heavens, told us the secrets of the stars, the glories of the constellations—the geologists who found the story of the world in fossil forms, in memoranda kept in ancient rocks, in lines written by waves, by frost and fire—the anatomists who sought in muscle, nerve and bone for all the mysteries of life—the chemists who unraveled Nature's work that they might learn her art—the physicians who have laid the hand of science on the brow of pain, the hand whose magic touch restores—the surgeons who have defeated Nature's self and forced her to preserve the lives of those she labored to destroy.

I thank the discoverers of chloroform and ether, the two angels who give to their beloved sleep, and wrap the throbbing brain in the soft robes of dreams. I thank the great inventors—those who gave us movable type and the press, by means of which great thoughts and all discovered facts are made immortal—the inventors of engines, of the great ships, of the railways, the cables and telegraphs. I thank the great mechanics, the workers in iron and steel, in wood and stone. I thank the inventors and makers of the numberless things of use and luxury.

I thank the industrious men, the loving mothers, the useful women. They are the benefactors of our race.

The inventor of pins did a thousand times more good than all the popes and cardinals, the bishops and priests—than all the clergymen and parsons, exhorters and theologians that ever lived.

The inventor of matches did more for the comfort and convenience of mankind than all the founders of religions and the makers of all creeds—than all malicious monks and selfish saints.

I thank the honest men and women who have expressed their sincere thoughts, who have been true to themselves and have preserved the veracity of their souls.

I thank the thinkers of Greece and Rome, Zeno and Epicurus, Cicero and Lucretius.— I thank Bruno, the bravest, and Spinoza, the subtlest of men.

I thank Voltaire, whose thought lighted a flame in the brain of man, unlocked the doors of superstition's cells and gave liberty to many millions of his fellowmen. Voltaire —a name that sheds light. Voltaire—

a star that superstition's darkness cannot quench.

I thank the great poets—the dramatists. I thank Homer and Aeschylus, and I thank Shakespeare above them all. I thank Burns for the heart-throbs he changed into songs, for his lyrics of flame. I thank Shelley for his Skylark. Keats for his Grecian Urn and Byron for his Prisoner of Chillon. I thank the great novelists. I thank the great sculptors. I thank the unknown man who moulded and chiseled the Venus de Milo. I thank the great painters. I thank Rembrandt and Corot. I thank all who have adorned, enriched and ennobled life—all who have created the great, the noble, the heroric and artistic ideals.

I thank the statesmen who have preserved the rights of man. I thank Paine whose genius sowed the seeds of independence in the hearts of '76. I thank Jefferson whose mighty words for liberty have made the circuit of the globe. I thank the founders, the defenders, the saviours of the Republic. I thank Ericson, the greatest mechanic of his century, for the monitor. I thank Lincoln for the Proclamation. I thank Grant for his victories and the vast host that fought for the right,—for the freedom of man. I thank them all—the living and the dead.

I thank the great scientists—those who have reached the foundation, the bed rock—who have built upon facts—the great scientists, in whose presence theologians look silly and feel malicious.

The scientists never persecuted, never imprisoned their fellowmen. They forged no chains, built no dungeons, erected no scaffolds—tore no flesh with red hot pincers—dislocated no joints on racks—crushed no bones in iron boots—extinguished no eyes—tore out no tongues and lighted no fagots. They did not pretend to be inspired—did not claim to be prophets or saints or to have been born again. They were only intelligent and honest men. They did not appeal to force or fear. They did not regard men as slaves to be ruled by torture, by lash and chain, nor as children to be cheated with illusions, rocked in the cradle of an idiot creed and soothed by a lullaby of lies.

They did not wound—they healed. They did not kill—they lengthened life. They did not enslave—they broke the chains and made men free. They sowed the seeds of knowledge and many millions have reaped, are reaping, and will reap the harvest of joy.

I thank Humboldt and Helmholtz and Haeckel and Büchner. I thank Lamarck and Darwin—Darwin who revolutionized the thought of the intellectual world. I thank Huxley and Spencer. I thank the scientists one and all.

I thank the heroes, the destroyers of prejudice and fear—the dethroners of savage gods—the extinguishers of hate's eternal fire—the heroes, the breakers of chains—the founders of free states—the makers of just laws—the heroes who fought and fell on countless fields—the heroes whose dungeons became shrines

—the heroes whose blood made scaffolds sacred—the heroes, the apostles of reason, the disciples of truth, the soldiers of freedom—the heroes who held high the holy torch and filled the world with light.

With all my heart I thank them all.

TRIBUTE TO HENRY WARD BEECHER.

HENRY WARD BEECHER was born in a Puritan penitentiary, of which his father was one of the wardens—a prison with very narrow and closely-grated windows. Under its walls were the rayless, hopeless and measureless dungeons of the damned, and on its roof fell the shadow of God's eternal frown. In this prison the creed and catechism were primers for children, and from a pure sense of duty their loving hearts were stained and scarred with the religion of John Calvin.

In those days the home of an orthodox minister was an inquisition in which babes were tortured for the good of their souls. Children then, as now, rebelled against the infamous absurdities and cruelties of the creed.

No Calvinist was ever able, unless with blows, to answer the questions of his child. Children were raised in what was called "the nurture and admonition of the Lord"—that is to say, their wills were broken or subdued, their natures were deformed and dwarfed, their desires defeated or destroyed, and their development arrested or perverted. Life was robbed of its Spring, its Summer and its Autumn. Children stepped from the cradle into the snow. No laughter, no sunshine, no joyous, free, unburdened days. God, an infinite detective, watched them from above, and Satan, with malicious leer, was waiting for their souls below. Between these monsters life was passed. Infinite consequences were predicated of the smallest action, and a burden greater than a God could bear was placed upon the heart and brain of every child. To think, to ask questions, to doubt, to investigate, were acts of rebellion. To express pity for the lost, writhing in the dungeons below, was simply to give evidence that the enemy of souls had been at work within their hearts.

Among all the religions of this world—from the creed of cannibals who devoured flesh, to that of Calvinists who polluted souls—there is none, there has been none, there will be none, more utterly heartless and inhuman than was the orthodox Congregationalism of New England in the year of grace 1813. It despised every natural joy, hated pictures, abhorred statues as lewd and lustful things, execrated music, regarded nature as fallen and corrupt, man as totally depraved and woman as somewhat worse. The theatre was the vestibule of perdition, actors the servants of Satan, and Shakespeare a trifling wretch, whose words were seeds of death. And yet the virtues found a welcome, cordial and sincere; duty was done as understood; obligations were discharged; truth was told; self-denial was practised for the sake of others, and many hearts were good and true in spite of book and creed.

In this atmosphere of theological miasma, in this hideous dream of superstition, in this penitentiary, moral and austere, this babe first saw the imprisoned gloom. The natural desires ungratified, the laughter suppressed, the logic brow-beaten by authority, the humor frozen by fear—of many generations—were in this child, a child destined to rend and wreck the prison's walls.

Through the grated windows of his cell, this child, this boy, this man, caught glimpses of the outer world, of fields and skies. New thoughts were in his brain, new hopes within his heart. Another heaven bent above his life. There came a revelation of the beautiful and real. Theology grew mean and small. Nature wooed and won and saved this mighty soul.

Her countless hands were sowing seeds within his tropic brain. All sights and sounds—all colors, forms and fragments— were stored within the treasury of his mind. His thoughts were moulded by the graceful curves of streams, by winding paths in woods, the charm of quiet country roads, and lanes grown indistinct with weeds and grass—by vines that cling and hide with leaf and flower the crumbling wall's decay—by cattle standing in the summer pools like statues of content.

There was within his words the subtle spirit of the season's change—of everything that is, of everything that lies between the slumbering seeds, that, half-awakened by the April rain, have dreams of heaven's blue, and feel the amorous kisses of the sun, and that strange tomb wherein the alchemist doth give to death's cold dust the throb and thrill of life again. He saw with loving eyes the willows of the meadow-streams grow red beneath the glance of Spring—the grass along the marsh's edge—the stir of life beneath the withered leaves—the moss below the drip of snow—the flowers that give their bosoms to the first south wind that wooes—the sad and timid violets that only bear the gaze of love from eyes half closed—the ferns, where fancy gives a thousand forms with but a single plan—the green and sunny slopes enriched with daisy's silver and the cowslip's gold.

As in the leafless woods some tree, aflame with life, stands like a rapt poet in the heedless crowd, so stood this man among his fellowmen.

All there is of leaf and bud, of flower and fruit, of painted insect life, and all the winged and happy children of the air that Summer holds beneath her dome of blue, were known and loved by him. He loved the yellow Autumn fields, the golden stacks, the happy homes of men, the orchard's bending boughs, the sumach's flags of flame, the maples with transfigured leaves, the tender yellow of the beech, the wondrous harmonies of brown and gold—the vines where hang the clustered spheres of wit and mirth. He loved the winter days, the whirl and drift of snow—all forms of frost—the rage and fury of the storm, when in the forest, desolate and stripped, the brave old pine towers green and grand—a prophecy of Spring. He heard the rhythmic sounds of Nature's busy strife, the hum of bees, the songs of birds, the eagle's cry, the murmur of the streams, the sighs and lamentations of the winds, and all the voices of the sea. He loved the shores, the vales, the crags and cliffs, the city's busy streets, the introspective, silent plain, the solemn splendors of the night, the silver sea of dawn, and evening's clouds of molten gold. The love of Nature freed this loving man.

One by one the fetters fell; the gratings disappeared, the sunshine smote the roof, and on the floors of stone light streamed from open doors. He realized the darkness and despair, the cruelty and hate, the starless blackness of the old, maglignant creed. The flower of pity grew and blossomed in his heart. The selfish "consolation" filled his eyes with tears. He saw that what is called the Christian's hope is, that, among the countless billions wrecked and lost, a meagre few perhaps may reach the eternal shore—a hope that, like the desert rain, gives neither leaf nor bud—a hope that gives no joy, no peace, to any great and loving soul. It is the dust on which the serpent feeds that coils in heartless breasts.

Day by day the wrath and vengeance faded from the sky—the Jewish God grew vague and dim—the threats of torture and eternal pain grew vulgar and absurd, and all the miracles seemed strangely out of place. They clad the Infinite in motley garb, and gave to aureoled heads the cap and bells.

Touched by the pathos of all human life, knowing the shadows that fall on every heart—the thorns in every path, the sighs, the sorrows, and the tears that lie between a mother's arms and death's embrace—this great and gifted man denounced, denied, and damned with all his heart the fanged and frightful dogma that souls were made to feed the eternal hunger—ravenous as famine—of a God's revenge.

Take out this fearful, fiendish, heartless lie—compared with which all other lies are true—and the great arch of orthodox religion crumbling falls.

To the average man the Christian hell and heaven are only words. He has no scope of thought. He lives but in a dim, impoverished now. To him the past is dead—the future still unborn. He occupies with downcast eyes that narrow line of barren, shifting sand that lies between the flowing seas. But Genius knows all time. For him the dead all live and breathe, and act their countless parts again. All human life is in his now, and every moment feels the thrill of all to be.

No one can overestimate the good accomplished by this marvelous, many-sided man. He helped to slay the heart-devouring monster of the Christian world. He tried to civilize the church, to humanize the creeds, to soften pious breasts of stone, to take the fear from mothers' hearts, the chains of creed from every brain, to put the star of hope in every sky and over every grave. Attacked on every side, maligned by those who preached the law of love, he wavered not, but fought whole-hearted to the end.

Obstruction is but virtue's foil. From thwarted light leaps color's flame. The stream impeded has a song.

He passed from harsh and cruel creeds to that serene philosophy that has no place for pride or hate, that threatens no revenge, that looks on sin as stumblings of the blind and pities those who fall, knowing that in the souls of all there is a sacred yearning for the light. He ceased to think of man as something thrust upon the world—an exile from some other sphere. He felt at last that men are part of Nature's self—kindred of all life—the gradual growth of countless years; that all the sacred books were helps until outgrown, and all religions, rough and devious paths that man has worn with weary feet in sad and painful search for truth and peace. To him these paths were wrong, and yet all gave the promise of success. He knew that all the streams, no matter how they wander, turn and curve amid the hills or rocks, or linger in the lakes and pools, must some time reach the sea. These views enlarged his soul and made him patient with the world, and while the wintry snows of age were falling on his head, Spring, with all her wealth of bloom, was in his heart.

The memory of this ample man is now a part of Nature's wealth. He battled for the rights of men. His heart was with the slave. He stood against the selfish greed of millions banded to protect the pirate's trade. His voice was for the right when freedom's friends were few. He taught the church to think and doubt. He did not fear to stand alone. His brain took counsel of his heart. To every foe he offered reconcilation's hand. He loved this land of ours, and added to its glory through the world. He was the greatest orator that stood within the pulpit's narrow curve. He loved the liberty of speech. There was no trace of bigot in his blood. He was a brave and generous man.

With reverent hands, I place this tribute on his tomb.

AN ENTIRELY NEW EDITION.

THE
Writings of Col. R. G. Ingersoll.

VOLUME ONE NOW READY.

Volume 1. Large octavo, 1431 pages, wide margins, large and handsome type; fine steel portrait; elegantly bound in cloth, gold back and side stamps; marble edges; half morocco, full sheep, library style.

THE friends and admirers of Mr. Ingersoll's writings have long wanted just such a work as this. Hitherto, the publisher has been content with issuing each lecture, argument and other production separately. This volume brings together no less than nineteen of the Colonel's famous lectures on religious and patriotic subjects, and several of the orations, tributes and selections that have become classics in literature. It is a delight to find them here in such admirable and ready form for preservation and reference. The edition will doubtless soon be exhausted, and a second volume is promised that will lay the public under new obligation. A third, fourth, fifth, or sixth volume, each equally valuable, would not cover all Col. Ingersoll's writings and sayings, and those who treat themselves to a copy of this first volume will want to see the series completed—will not be happy until it is.

CONTENTS OF VOLUME 1.

The Gods; Humboldt; Individuality; Thomas Paine; Heretics and Heresies; The Ghosts; The Liberty of Man, Woman and Child; The Centennial Oration, or Declaration of Independence, July 4th, 1876. What I Know About Farming in Illinois; Speech at Cincinnati in 1876, nominating James G. Blaine for the Presidency; The Past Rises Before Me; or, Vision of War, an extract from a Speech made at the Soldiers and Sailors Reunion at Indianapolis, Indiana, Sept. 21, 1876; A Tribute to Ebon C. Ingersoll; The Grant Banquet; Crimes Against Criminals; Tribute to the Rev. Alexander Clarke. Some Mistakes of Moses; What Must We Do to be Saved? Blasphemy, Argument in the trial of C. B. Reynolds. Six Interviews with Robert G. Ingersoll on Six Sermons by the Rev. T. DeWitt Talmage, D. D.; to which is added a Talmagian Catechism, and four Prefaces, which contain some of Mr. Ingersoll's best and brightest sayings.

Price, postpaid, cloth $3.50; half morocco $5.00; full sheep $5.00.

Size of volume 10¼ x 7¼ x 2½, weight 6½ lbs.

C. P. FARRELL,

(Only authorized publisher of Col. Ingersoll's books.

NEW YORK.

(OVER.)

New Books by Col. R. G. Ingersoll.

"About the Holy Bible." New Lecture. Paper, 25 cts.
Foundations of Faith. A New Lecture. Paper, 25 cts.
Some Reasons Why. A New Lecture. Paper, 25 cts.
Myth and Miracle. Now published for the first time. Paper, 25 cts.
Which Way? A New Lecture, revised and enlarged. Paper, 25 cts.
Ingersoll's Great Lecture on Shakespeare. A Masterpiece, containing a handsome half-tone likeness of Shakespeare from the Kesselstadt death mask. "Shakespeare was an intellectual ocean whose waves touched all the shores of thought." Paper, 25 cts.; cloth, 50 cts.
Abraham Lincoln. Containing a handsome portrait, "A piece of sublime eulogy." Paper, 25 cts.
Voltaire. With portrait, "He was the greatest man of his century, and did more to free the human race than any other of the sons of men." Paper, 25 cts.
Liberty for Man, Woman and Child. Has a fine photo-engraving of the Colonel and both his grandchildren, Eva and Robert; also the *TRIBUTE TO HIS BROTHER.* Paper, 25 cts.
The Great Ingersoll Controversy. Containing the Famous Christmas Sermon, by R. G. Ingersoll. Paper, 25 cts.
Is Suicide a Sin? Ingersoll's startling, brilliant and thrillingly eloquent letters, which created such a sensation when published in the *New York World*, together with the replies of famous clergymen and writers. Paper, 25 cts.
"Prose-Poems and Selections." A new and cheap edition, containing over 400 pages. The most elegant volume in Liberal literature. Good paper, wide margins, plain cloth, (sixth edition.) Price, $1.50.
Two Patriotic Addresses. *THE REUNION ADDRESS* at Elmwood, Ills., September 5th, 1895, and the *DECORATION-DAY ORATION* in New York, May 30th, 1882. Both in one book. Paper, 25 cts.; cloth, 50 cts.
The Centennial Oration on the Declaration of Independence, July 4th, 1876, and the "*VISION OF WAR*," in one neat pamphlet. 10 cts.
God in the Constitution. One of the best papers Colonel Ingersoll ever wrote. Price, 10 cts.
The Christian Religion. By Col. R. G. Ingersoll and Judge Jeremiah S. Black. Paper, 25 cts.; cloth, 50 cts.
The Field=Ingersoll Discussion. Faith or Agnosticism? Paper, 25 cts.; cloth, 50 cts.
The Ingersoll-Gladstone Discussion on Christianity. Never before published in book form. Paper, 25 cts.; cloth, 50 cts.
"Life of Jesus Critically Examined," by David Friedrich Strauss. This edition is translated from the fourth German edition by George Eliot, and contains 784 large octavo pages of solid reading. This is a very valuable work, one which the church wishes had never been written, but which it cannot controvert. One volume, $4.50. (Now out of print and very hard to get.) Never sold before for less than $9.00.

SPECIAL NOTICE.

I have a few copies of Col. Ingersoll's speech on "Hard Times and the Way Out," price, paper, 20 cts. Also a few copies of the "Conkling Memorial," with fine steel engraving. Price, cloth, 50 cts.

Any or all the above Books sent prepaid upon receipt of price.

C. P. FARRELL, PUBLISHER,
220 Madison Avenue, New York.

www.ingramcontent.com/pod-product-compliance
Lightning Source LLC
Chambersburg PA
CBHW020323090426
42735CB00009B/1373